EDLE stumble ZOOMB rap Ping TAP berj HOWL
atter HOWL tap Flap flap ra P
SWISH Boo splatter drip TUMBLE TAP SLO de swis. ziggildy click
LOW PING wiggle tingle clickety-clack o Boo SPLASH SPLISH TAP TA
SH plop clap WHISTLE ROAR click clickety-clack squiggle dunder drip
ping SLISH bong TAP TAP BANG clap CLAN
RUMBLE clang drop BASH clapcla
shag ping PUMP-A-RUM SLOSH A GALOSH BONG flop
H-PA-RAH flip flop Slurp THUNDER SLITHER PING Boo tingle
slip slap plip bang clatter rat
Hoot clang WIGGLE stumble
wl blunder tootle-too slurp flap TOOT HOOT clap PICKLE-PE
LE clunk QUIVER tap tap CRASH HOOT clunk
YOWL rap slosh CLANG SWASH slip slap plip
ckety-clack scatter drip drop SWISH slosh rattle batter TH
ONG clang clap THUMP TAP WIGGLE BASH Whisc
YOWL swish bber Too whistle TOOT IGGLE SLU PUMP BONG Q
BOO R HOOT

for Michael Smith

Oxford University Press, Walton Street, Oxford OX2 6DP

Oxford New York Toronto
Delhi Bombay Calcutta Madras Karachi
Petaling Jaya Singapore Hong Kong Tokyo
Nairobi Dar es Salaam Cape Town
Melbourne Auckland

and associated companies in

Berlin Ibadan

Oxford is a trade mark of Oxford University Press

Illustrations © Nick Sharratt 1987

Selection, arrangement and editorial matter
© Oxford University Press 1987

First published 1987
Reprinted 1988, 1989 (twice), 1990, 1992

First published in paperback 1989
Reprinted 1989, 1990, 1992

British Library Cataloguing in Publication Data

Noisy poems.—(Umbrella series)
1. Children's poetry, English
I. Bennett, Jill,
II. Sharrat, Nick
III. Series
821'.914'0809282   PR1195.C47

ISBN 0–19–276063–7 (Hardback)
ISBN 0–19–278219–3 (Paperback)

The editor and publisher are grateful for permission to reprint the following copyright poems.

Elizabeth Coatsworth: 'Rhyme'. Copyright © 1960 Elizabeth Coatsworth. Eleanor Farjeon: 'J is for Jazz-Man' from *Silver Sand and Snow* (Michael Joseph). Reprinted by permission of David Higham Associates Limited. Jimmy Garthwaite: 'Engineers' from *Puddin' An' Pie*, copyright 1929 by Harper & Row Publishers, Inc. Renewed 1957 by Merle Garthwaite. Reprinted by permission of Harper & Row, Publishers, Inc. Dahlov Ipcar: 'Fishes Evening Song' from *Whisperings and Other Things* (Alfred A Knopf, 1967), copyright © 1967 by Dahlov Ipcar. Reprinted by permission of McIntosh and Otis, Inc. David McCord: 'Song of the Train' from *One At A Time*, copyright 1952 by David McCord. Reprinted by permission of Little, Brown and Company. Eve Merriam: 'Weather' from *Catch a Little Rhyme*, copyright © 1966 by Eve Merriam. Reprinted by permission of the author. All rights reserved. Spike Milligan: 'On the Ning Nang Nong' from *Silly Verse For Kids and Animals* (Michael Joseph Ltd.). Reprinted by permission of Spike Milligan Productions Ltd. Tao Lang Pee: 'Sampan', published in *Wheel Around the World* (ed. Chris Searle, Macdonald & Co.). Jack Prelutsky: 'Spaghetti! Spaghetti!' from *Rainy Rainy Saturday*, copyright © 1980 by Jack Prelutsky; 'The Yak' from *Zoo Doings*, copyright © 1967, 1983 by Jack Prelutsky. Both reprinted by permission of Greenwillow Books (A Division of William Morrow & Company). Barbara Ireson: 'The Small Ghostie' from *Rhyme Time* (Hamlyn), copyright Barbara Ireson. Used by permission of the author. James Reeves: 'The Ceremonial Band' from *James Reeves: The Complete Poems*, © James Reeves Estate. Reprinted by permission of the James Reeves Estate.

We have failed in two instances to contact the copyright holder. If notified, the publisher will be pleased to make necessary corrections in future editions.

Typeset by Oxford Publishing Services

Printed in Hong Kong

NOISY POEMS

COLLECTED BY JILL BENNETT

ILLUSTRATED BY NICK SHARRATT

OXFORD UNIVERSITY PRESS

THE CEREMONIAL BAND

(To be said out loud by a chorus and solo voices)

The old King of Dorchester,
He had a little orchestra,
And never did you hear such a
                    ceremonial band.
  'Tootle-too,' said the flute,
  'Deed-a-reedle,' said the fiddle,
For the fiddles and the flutes were
                    the finest in the land.

The old King of Dorchester,
He had a little orchestra,
And never did you hear such a
                    ceremonial band.
  'Pump-a-rum,' said the drum,
  'Tootle-too,' said the flute,
  'Deed-a-reedle,' said the fiddle,
For the fiddles and the flutes were
                    the finest in the land.

The old King of Dorchester,
He had a little orchestra,
And never did you hear such a
                    ceremonial band.
  'Pickle-pee,' said the fife,
  'Pump-a-rum,' said the drum,
  'Tootle-too,' said the flute,
  'Deed-a-reedle,' said the fiddle,
For the fiddles and the flutes were
                    the finest in the land.

The old King of Dorchester,
He had a little orchestra,
And never did you hear such a
                    ceremonial band.
  'Zoomba-zoom,' said the bass,
  'Pickle-pee,' said the fife,
  'Pump-a-rum,' said the drum,
  'Tootle-too,' said the flute,
  'Deed-a-reedle,' said the fiddle,
For the fiddles and the flutes were
                    the finest in the land.

The old King of Dorchester,
He had a little orchestra,
And never did you hear such a
                    ceremonial band.
  'Pah-pa-rah,' said the trumpet,
  'Zoomba-zoom,' said the bass,
  'Pickle-pee,' said the fife,
  'Pump-a-rum,' said the drum,
  'Tootle-too,' said the flute,
  'Deed-a-reedle,' said the fiddle,
For the fiddles and the flutes were
                    the finest in the land,
Oh! the fiddles and the flutes were
                    the finest in the land!

James Reeves

ON THE NING NANG NONG

On the Ning Nang Nong
Where the Cows go Bong!
And the Monkeys all say Boo!
There's a Nong Nang Ning
Where the trees go Ping!
And the tea pots Jibber Jabber Joo.
On the Nong Ning Nang
All the mice go Clang!
And you can't catch 'em when they do!
So it's Ning Nang Nong!
Cows go Bong!
Nong Nang Ning!
Trees go Ping!
Nong Ning Nang!
The mice go Clang!
What a noisy place to belong,
Is the Ning Nang Ning Nang Nong!

Spike Milligan

SONG OF THE TRAIN

Clickety-clack,
Wheels on the track,
This is the way
They begin the attack:
Click-ety-clack,
Click-ety-clack,
Click-ety, *clack-ety,*
Click-ety
Clack.

Clickety-clack,
Over the crack,
Faster and faster
The song of the track:
Clickety-clack,
Clickety-clack,
Clickety, clackety,
Clackety
Clack.

Riding in front,
Riding in back,
Everyone hears
The song of the track:
Clickety-clack
Clickety-clack,
Clickety-*clickety*
Clackety
Clack.

David McCord

SAMPAN

Waves lap lap
Fish fins clap clap
Brown sails flap flap
Chop-sticks tap tap
Up and down the long green river
Ohe Ohe lanterns quiver
Willow branches brush the river
Ohe Ohe lanterns quiver
Waves lap lap
Fish fins clap clap
Brown sails flap flap
Chop-sticks tap tap

Tao Lang Pee

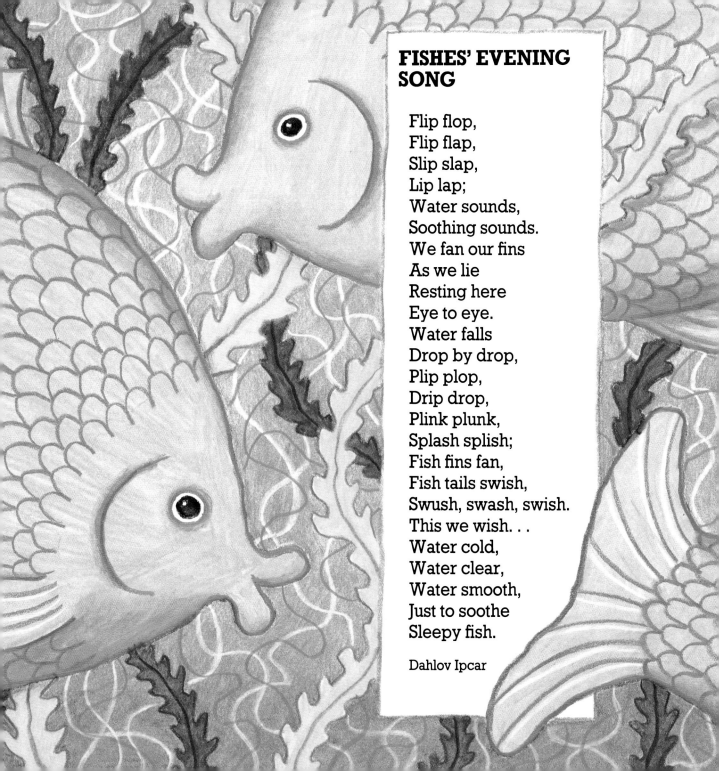

FISHES' EVENING SONG

Flip flop,
Flip flap,
Slip slap,
Lip lap;
Water sounds,
Soothing sounds.
We fan our fins
As we lie
Resting here
Eye to eye.
Water falls
Drop by drop,
Plip plop,
Drip drop,
Plink plunk,
Splash splish;
Fish fins fan,
Fish tails swish,
Swush, swash, swish.
This we wish. . .
Water cold,
Water clear,
Water smooth,
Just to soothe
Sleepy fish.

Dahlov Ipcar

SPAGHETTI! SPAGHETTI!

Spaghetti! spaghetti!
you're wonderful stuff,
I love you, spaghetti,
I can't get enough.
You're covered with sauce
and you're sprinkled with cheese,
spaghetti! spaghetti!
oh, give me some more please.

Spaghetti! spaghetti!
piled high in a mound,
you wiggle, you wriggle,
you squiggle around.
There's slurpy spaghetti
all over my plate,
spaghetti! spaghetti!
I think you are great.

Spaghetti! spaghetti!
I love you a lot,
you're slishy, you're sloshy,
delicious and hot.
I gobble you down
oh, I can't get enough,
spaghetti! spaghetti!
you're wonderful stuff.

Jack Prelutsky

RHYME

I like to see a thunder storm,
A dunder storm,
A blunder storm,
I like to see it, black and slow
Come stumbling down the hills.

I like to hear a thunder storm,
  A plunder storm,
    A wonder storm,
Roar loudly at our little house
And shake the window sills!

Elizabeth Coatsworth

WEATHER

Dot a dot dot   dot a dot dot
Spotting the window-pane.
Spack a spack speck   flick a flack fleck
Freckling the window-pane.

A spatter a scatter   a wet cat a clatter
A splatter a rumble outside.
Umbrella umbrella umbrella umbrella
Bumbershoot barrel of rain.

Slosh a galosh   slosh a galosh
Slither and slather and glide
A puddle a jump a puddle a jump
A puddle a jump puddle splosh
A juddle a pump aluddle a dump a
Puddmuddle jump in and slide!

Eve Merriam

JAZZ-MAN

Crash and
                    CLANG!
Bash and
                    BANG!

And up in the road the Jazz-Man sprang!
The One-Man-Jazz-Band playing in the street,
Drums with his Elbows, Cymbals with his Feet,
Pipes with his Mouth, Accordion with his Hand,
Playing all his Instruments to Beat the Band!

TOOT and
                    Tingle!
HOOT and
                    Jingle!

Oh, what a Clatter! How the tunes all mingle!
Twenty Children couldn't make as much Noise *as*
The Howling Pandemonium of the One-Man-Jazz!

Eleanor Farjeon

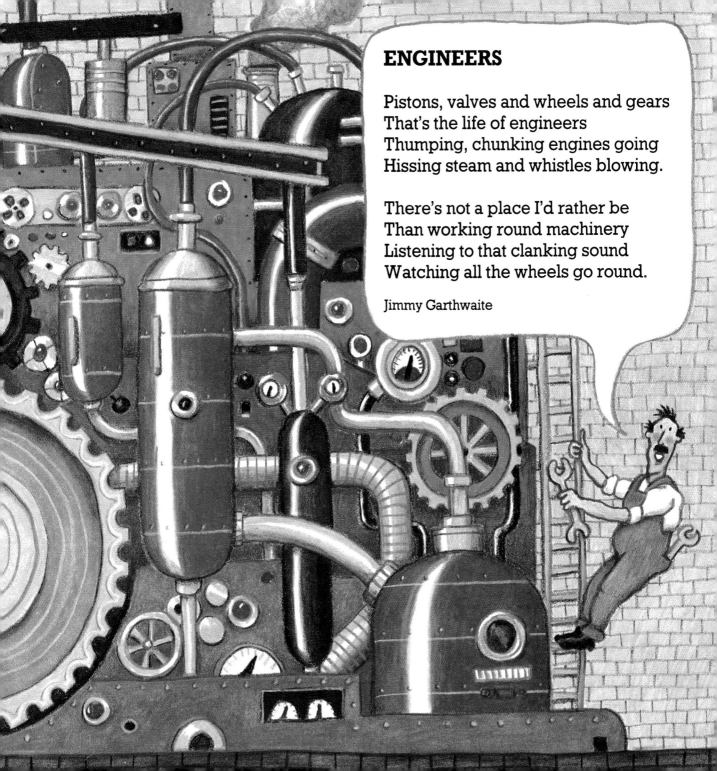

ENGINEERS

Pistons, valves and wheels and gears
That's the life of engineers
Thumping, chunking engines going
Hissing steam and whistles blowing.

There's not a place I'd rather be
Than working round machinery
Listening to that clanking sound
Watching all the wheels go round.

Jimmy Garthwaite

THE YAK

Yickity-yackity, yickity-yak,
the yak has a scriffily, scraffily back;
some yaks are brown yaks and some yaks are black,
yickity-yackity, yickity-yak.

Sniggildy-snaggildy, sniggildy-snag,
the yak is all covered with shiggildy-shag;
he walks with a ziggildy-zaggildy-zag,
sniggildy-snaggildy, sniggildy-snag.

Yickity-yackity, yickity-yak,
the yak has a scriffily, scraffily back;
some yaks are brown yaks and some yaks are black,
yickity-yackity, yickity-yak.

Jack Prelutsky

THE SMALL GHOSTIE

When it's late and it's dark
And everyone sleeps. . . shhh shhh shhh,
Into our kitchen
A small ghostie creeps. . . shhh shhh shhh.

We hear knocking and raps
And then rattles and taps,

Then he clatters and clangs
And he batters and bangs,

And he whistles and yowls
And he screeches and howls. . .

So we pull up our covers over our heads
And we block up our ears and WE STAY IN OUR BEDS

Barbara Ireson

SPLASH jingle TAP HOOT plip slish slos

Tickety HISS rap ping slosh hoot knock FLOP BANG sniggildy

TOOTLE-TOO click clap BATTER plop clunk clack toot PLINK PLUNK clap

ping boo Yickity-yak plip Toot SLIP SLAP rap slap BOO plop

BONG slurp flip thump BOO RATTLE slosh a galos

zoomba-zoom SLITHER clap boo BONG clang chop du

KNOCK flop shake JIBBER THUNDER plop SLURP BO

BANG GOBBLE clang pump-a-rum plip plop JABBER ping shigg

SCREECH BONG ping lap lap thump CLANK boo pickle-pee TAP crac

cingle TOOT BASH JINGLE plop BONG rap CLANG

FLICK A FLACK spatter slosh TOOT sniggildy-snag bong SQUI

cingle clunk splosh HOWL

ash splish splash BANG HOOT slish CRASH slop FLIP FLOP clap tootle-too his

SWASH thunder HOOT clunk BON

SNIGGILDY slurp SQUIGGLE thunder CLICKETY-CLACK YAK tap clunk SCREE

TAP slosh scatter YICKITY YAK plip plop LATHER howl